mummy
& me
bake

LONDON, NEW YORK, MUNICH, MELBOURNE, DELHI

Project editor Laura Palosuo
Senior designer Hannah Moore
Photographer Will Heap
Home economist Denise Smart
Illustrator Helen Dodsworth
Senior producer (pre-production) Tony Phipps
Producer Stephanie McConnell
Jacket designer Claire Patane
Creative technical support Sonia Charbonnier
Managing editor Penny Smith
Managing art editor Marianne Markham
Art director Jane Bull
Publisher Mary Ling

First published in Great Britain in 2015 by
Dorling Kindersley Limited,
80 Strand, London WC2R 0RL
1 2 3 4 5 6 7 8 9 10
001–192950–02/15

A CIP catalogue record for this book
is available from the British Library.

ISBN: 978-0-2411-8226-0
Printed and bound in China by Hung Hing.

Discover more at
www.dk.com

Contents

 This symbol tells you that this is a "find out more" page.
These pages give you additional baking facts.

Baking basics

Baking is lots of fun and with this book you will learn to make all kinds of yummy treats. To make sure you stay safe in the kitchen, here are a few important rules. Always be careful and follow the instructions.

Kitchen rules

• When you're in the kitchen, you should ask an adult to move things in and out of the oven and heat things on the hob.
• Ask an adult to help if you need to use a sharp knife or an electrical appliance.
• Wash your hands before and after you work with food. Always wash your hands after handling raw eggs and raw meat.
• Do not lick your fingers after you've worked with food.
• Check the use-by date on all ingredients.
• Follow the instructions on packaging on how to store food.
• The dessert-type recipes are meant as a special treat so eat them as part of a balanced diet.

Getting started

1. Read the instructions all the way through before you start.
2. Gather together everything you need.
3. Have a cloth handy to mop up spillages.
4. Put on an apron, tie back your hair, and wash your hands.

 ## Safety

All the projects in this book are t be made under adult supervision. When you see the warning triang take extra care as hot cookers, electric appliances, and sharp implements are used in making a recipe. Ask an adult to help you.

Key to symbol

Prep time
How long will it take to prepare

Cook time
How long will it take to cook in the oven

Yield
How many piec or servings it will make

Clean hands

Basic baking kit

Here's equipment that's often used in baking. You'll need to use some of these items to make the recipes in this book.

Flour shaker

Sieve

Cake tins

Paper cases

Muffin tin

Greaseproof paper

Rolling pin

Spoons

Baking tray

Pastry brush

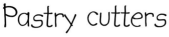

Electric whisk

Pastry cutters

Cooling rack

Apron

Mixing bowl

Weighing and measuring

Baking is chemistry in the kitchen. You need to get the amounts just right for the recipes to work as planned. There are many different ways to measure ingredients.

Measuring spoons are used for measuring small amounts accurately.

Measuring cups are used in some countries to measure dry ingredients.

Use a knife to level off the cup to make sure you measure the right amount.

tsp = teaspoon   tbsp = tablespoon

Cups

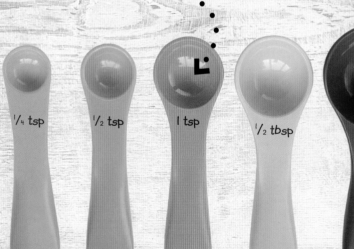

¼ tsp   ½ tsp   1 tsp   ½ tbsp   1 tbsp

Imperial measures

oz = ounce, lb = pound
There are 16 ounces in a pound.

Metric measures

g = gram, kg = kilogram
There are 1,000 grams in a kilogram.

Measuring around the world

Different countries use different systems for measuring. Recipe ingredients are measured using either the **metric** or **imperial** system. It doesn't matter which system you use – just make sure you don't mix up the systems within one recipe.

A kitchen scale can also be used to measure dry ingredients. Scales often show both metric and imperial units.

Measuring jugs are for measuring liquids. For an accurate measurement, make sure your eyes are level with the surface of the liquid.

Jugs are good for measuring liquids

Imperial measures

fl oz = fluid ounce

Metric measures

ml = millilitre
There are 1,000 millilitres in a litre

find out more Ingredient magic

Like magic, ordinary sugar, eggs, butter, and flour turn into biscuits in the oven. But did you know they all do different jobs? Here's what they each bring to the mix.

Sugar

Everyone knows that sugar adds sweetness, but it also makes biscuits browner and crunchier by caramelizing and absorbing moisture.

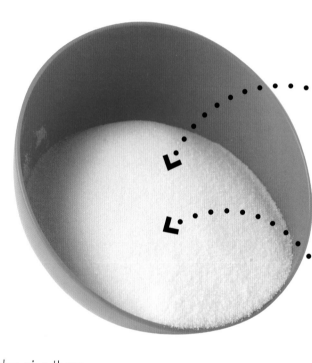

Makes biscuits turn brown

Makes biscuits crunchy

Eggs

Eggs help biscuits rise. They also give them structure because the liquid in eggs bonds with the flour and sets in the oven.

Helps biscuits rise

Gives biscuits structure

Adds flavour to biscuits

Helps make biscuits crumbly

Butter

Butter coats some of the flour in fat and protects it from the liquid in a recipe. This makes biscuits crumbly. Butter also adds flavour to biscuits.

Flour

The amount of flour in a recipe makes biscuits crumbly or chewy. When the proportion of flour is high, biscuits are crumblier. Less flour means chewier biscuits.

Makes biscuits chewy or crumbly depending on amount

Why do biscuits spread?

In the heat of the oven, the butter and sugar in biscuits melt. This helps the ball of biscuit dough spread out flat.

after baking

before baking

the ball of dough has spread out flat

Crunchy cut-out biscuits

This simple biscuit dough is quick and easy to make, leaving you plenty of time for the fun part – rolling it flat and cutting out shapes.

Cut out all your favour
golden. This recipe mak

.... Dragonfly

You will need

| 225g (8oz) butter, cut into cubes | 125g (4½oz) caster sugar | 1 egg yolk | 1 teaspoon vanilla extract | 275g (9¾oz) plain flour |

...apes and bake them until ...ough to share with friends.

Butterfly

Iced biscuits

These crunchy biscuits are delicious eaten just as they are, but you can also decorate them. Turn to pages 14-15 for colourful icing ideas.

Equipment

- Mixing bowl • Wooden spoon
- Sieve • Clingfilm
- Rolling pin • Cookie cutters
- Baking sheet • Palette knife
- Wire cooling rack

1 hour to make (including 30 minutes chilling)

8-10 minutes to cook

makes 30 biscuits (depending on cutters)

Making biscuit dough

Follow the steps to make the dough for your biscuits. It's as easy as 1, 2, 3, 4!

beat it

1 Beat the butter and sugar together in a bowl until the mixture is light and fluffy and changes colour slightly.

stir it

2 Add the egg yolk and vanilla extract and stir them in. Next sift in the flour and mix again to make a dough.

squeeze it

3 Using your hands, bring the dough together and mould it into a ball. If bits fall off just stick them on again until you have a solid ball.

wrap it up

4 Wrap your ball in clingfilm. Put it in the fridge and leave it to chill for 30 minutes before you start making your biscuits.

Making crunchy cut-out biscuits

roll it flat

1 Preheat the oven to 180°C (350°F/Gas 4) Dust your work surface
   with flour and roll out the dough to about ½cm (¼in) thick.

cut out shapes

2 Use cookie cutters to cut out your biscuits.
   Gather up the trimmings into a ball and roll
   it out again to make more biscuits.

3 Move the biscuit shapes onto a non-stick
   baking sheet. Bake them for 8–10 minutes,
   then move to a rack to cool.

Icing biscuits

Mix up some icing and add colourful sprinkles to turn your biscuits into delicious works of art.

 +  +  =

100g (3½oz) icing sugar

3 tsp water

A few drops of food colouring

coloured icing

1 Add water to the sugar a little at a time and mix it in. Then add the food colouring.

2 Use a small spoon to spread on the icing. Add sprinkles and leave the icing to harden.

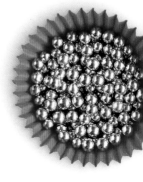

Use writing icing to add details and decoration.

Make just a few or a whole meadowful.

Equipment

- Butter knife • Clingfilm
- Rolling pin • Baking sheet
- Wire cooling rack

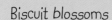

Biscuit blossoms

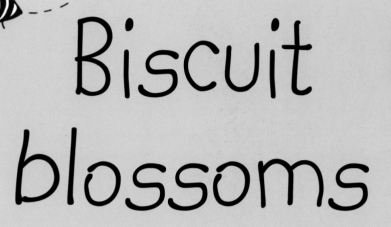

If these flowers look good enough to eat, it's because they are! You can make your swirly blossoms any colour you like by using different shades of food colouring.

You will need

Basic biscuit dough (see p.12)

A few drops of food colouring

1 tbsp cocoa powder

15 minutes to make (plus 15–30 minutes chilling)

12–14 minutes to cook

makes 26 biscuits

Making blossom biscuits

These steps show you how to make chocolate swirls and pink ones, but you can create any colour combination you like by adding your chosen colours in step 2.

divide it ⚠

wrap it up

1 Heat the oven to 180°C (350°F/Gas 4). Divide the dough into four equal pieces and shape them into balls.

2 Add a few drops of food colouring to one ball of dough and work it in. Knead the cocoa powder into another ball.

3 If the dough feels soft after mixing in the colours, wrap it in clingfilm and chill it in the fridge for 15–30 minutes.

roll the dough

4 Take a coloured ball of dough and roll it out into a rectangle. Roll out one of the plain balls to the same size.

5 Lay the plain-coloured rectangle on top of the coloured one, trimming off any excess. Roll the rectangles together lengthwise as shown.

slice it

6 Using a blunt knife, cut discs about ¹/₂cm (¹/₄in) thick from the roll. Then repeat steps 4–6 with the other two balls of dough.

7 Spread out the biscuits on a non-stick baking sheet and bake them for 12–14 minutes, then move to a wire rack to cool.

Go big!

Make giant swirly blossoms by rolling together all four balls of dough. Cut it into discs and bake as above.

Cookie machine

You will need

100g (3½oz)
butter, cubed

1 egg

125g (4½oz)
caster sugar

½ tsp vanilla
extract

150g (5½oz)
self-raising flour

Cookie factory

Turn your kitchen into your very own cookie factory and make lots of different kinds of cookies with this simple recipe. Then watch the orders come flooding in!

40 minutes to make (including 30 minutes chilling)	15 minutes to cook	makes 16 cookies

Equipment

• Large mixing bowl • Electric mixer or hand whisk • Wooden spoon • Sieve • 2 baking sheets • Baking parchment • Wire cooling rack

Cookie delivery

Box them up and send them to friends.

Making cookies

First make the dough, then add your toppings. You can mix and match them to make as many kinds of cookies as you like.

whisk

1 Preheat the oven to 180°C (350°F/Gas 4). Whisk the butter and egg together with a hand or electric whisk until light and fluffy.

2 Stir in the sugar and vanilla extract using a wooden spoon. Add the flour, sifting it in a little at a time.

3 Work the flour into the mixture with a wooden spoon until it forms a soft dough. Cover the bowl and put it in the fridge to chill for 30 minutes.

shape

4 Use your hands to shape the chilled dough into 16 balls. Space them out evenly on baking sheets lined with baking parchment.

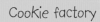

You can make different kinds of cookies at the same time – just add different toppings.

decorate

Making chocolate cookies

It's easy to turn your cookies into chocolate ones. Just mix two teaspoons of cocoa powder into the flour before you add it to the cookie dough in step 2.

5 Flatten the balls gently with your hand and press the toppings into the tops. Bake in the oven for 15 minutes, then transfer to a wire rack to cool.

Your cookies will spread out flat as they bake so be sure to leave plenty of space between them.

Plain chocolate

Double chocolate and marshmallow

find out
more

What happens in the oven?

Cake mixture goes in and, as if by magic, fluffy cake comes out. It's actually heat and a bit of chemistry that turn ingredients into cake.

Mmmm

⚠ Ovens are HOT! Take care near ovens and always ask an adult to move things in and out.

Don't open the door!

If you do, the cake may not rise properly, and it may even shrink! Heat helps the cake to rise by making the bubbles in the mixture bigger. Opening the door will lower the temperature in the oven and the bubbles will get smaller and the cake may sink. Never open the door until three fourths of the cooking time has passed.

Oven gloves

...mells good!

Pre-heating the oven

By heating the oven first you make sure that the temperature is right before the cake goes in.

How it works

When you make cake mixture, you cream butter and sugar together, which creates lots of little air bubbles. When egg and flour are added they surround these bubbles. In the heat of the oven, the bubbles get bigger and the cake mixture rises around them. When it gets hot enough, the egg and flour set (turn solid) and hold everything in place.

Small air bubbles

Big air bubbles

Watch the cake rise through the window

For a good result, set a timer.

Is it done?

Use a skewer, a toothpick, or even a strand of dried spaghetti to test your cake. The cake is ready when the tester comes out clean.

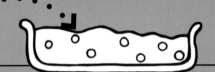

These cupcakes are...

Cupcake heaven

easy to make a

Soft, springy, light as air –
you might just float away in delight
when you bite into one of these
heavenly creations.

You will need

150g (5½oz)
sugar

150g (5½oz)
butter, cubed

3 eggs

1 tsp vanilla
extract

150g (5½oz)
self-raising flour

Equipment

• Mixing bowl • Electric mixer
• Small bowl • Fork • Sieve • Spatula
• 2 bun tins • 20 paper cases
• Spoon • Wire cooling rack

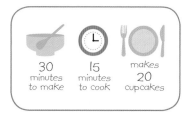

30
minutes
to make

15
minutes
to cook

makes
20
cupcakes

yummy you'll keep coming back for more.

Iced cakes

These cupcakes are delicious eaten just as they are, but you can also ice them. Turn to pages 30–33 for icing recipes and ideas.

The middles of the cupcakes rise up into high peaks.

Making cake mixture

It's important to cream the butter and sugar and beat the eggs well to get lots of air into the mixture. This will help your cakes rise.

beat the eggs

1 Cream the sugar and butter together in a bowl until light and fluffy.

2 In a separate bowl, beat the eggs and vanilla extract with a fork.

3 Pour in the egg mixture and combine it with the butter and sugar.

sift the flour

fold the mixture

4 Sift the flour into the bowl. You can tap the sieve with your hand to help the flour through.

5 Use a spatula to fold everything together. Do this carefully so you don't flatten the bubbles.

Making cupcakes

1 Preheat the oven to 180°C (350°F/Gas 4). Line two bun tins with 20 paper cases.

2 Use a spoon to divide the cake mixture between the cases.

you can ice the cakes once they're cool

3 Bake in the oven for 15 minutes until golden and just firm. Cool in the tins for 5 minutes, then move to a cooling rack.

Icing cupcakes

Icing sugar

Cut out a template and sift icing sugar over the top for a sweet and simple decoration.

1 tbsp icing sugar

⚠ **1** Using scissors, carefully cut out a template from baking parchment.

2 Hold the template in place and sift the icing sugar over the top.

Cream cheese icing

Use cream cheese to make a thick and creamy icing without any butter.

 200g (7oz) cream cheese + 2 tbsp icing sugar

1 Put the cream cheese and sugar into a medium-sized mixing bowl.

2 Mix them together until you have a creamy, spreadable icing.

Chocolate ganache

This elegant icing uses dark chocolate. For a sweeter taste, add sugar.

 225g (8oz) dark chocolate 250ml (9fl oz) double cream

Put the chocolate in a heatproof bowl. Bring the cream to the boil. As soon as it is at the boil, pour it over the chocolate.

Stir until the chocolate has melted and is fully mixed in. Set aside for 5 minutes. Then whisk until the ganache holds its shape.

Butter icing

Beat butter and sugar together to make a smooth, creamy icing.

 75g (3oz) butter, cubed 175g (6oz) icing sugar a few drops food colouring

Sift the icing sugar over the butter and mix it in with a wooden spoon.

Add food colouring and 1–2 tsp water and beat the mixture until it's fluffy.

Decorating cupcakes

Spread on some icing and add sprinkles, sweets, or fruit to make your own original cupcake creations.

Combine icing and sprinkles for a classic look.

coloured icing

Twit-twoo

butterfly cake

Cut the top off the cupcake and cut it in half. Spread on some icing and arrange the halves on top as wings.

marshmallow sheep

sprinkle

sprinkle

sprinkle

Use ganache or writing
icing to add details

spreading

Start in the middle of the
cake and spread on the icing
with the back of a spoon.

sweets

Cupcake art

It's time to let your imagination
run wild! Turn your cupcakes
into animals, bugs, or monsters
– or make beautiful individual
cakes fit for a princess. Look
on this page for ideas and
then design your own.

pretzel butterfly

15 minutes to make

30 minutes to cook

makes 8–10 portions

Spotty cake

Go wild and make a cake that's spotty like a leopard or stripy like a tiger. Then stand well clear of the feeding frenzy.

You will need

Basic cake mixture (see p.28)

2 tbsp cocoa powder

Equipment

- Baking parchment • Scissors
- 18cm (7in) round baking tin
- Tablespoon • Small sieve
- Butter knife

Making spotty cake

The spots in this cake are actually chocolate cake! It's made by adding cocoa powder to regular cake mixture. We do it in the same bowl so there's not too much washing up.

1 Preheat the oven to 180°C (350°F/Gas 4). Cut out a circle of baking parchment to fit your tin, then grease the tin and line it.

2 Drop spoonfuls of mixture into the tin, makin' sure you leave gaps between them. Stop whe you've used up half the mixture in the bowl.

3 Add the cocoa to the remaining mixture using a small sieve. If you end up with clumps in the sieve, break them up with the back of a spoon.

4 Mix the cocoa powder into the mixture with a spoon until it's smooth and glossy. This will make the spots or stripes in your cake.

5 Drop spoonfuls of the chocolate mixture into the gaps. Use a big spoon to make big spots or a smaller spoon for smaller spots.

Once cooked, turn the cake out onto a rack and let it cool before cutting it into 8–10 slices. Each slice will have a different jungle pattern.

6 To make stripes, drag a knife through the spots. Bake the cake for 30 minutes or until a wooden toothpick comes out clean.

Pineapple upside-down cake

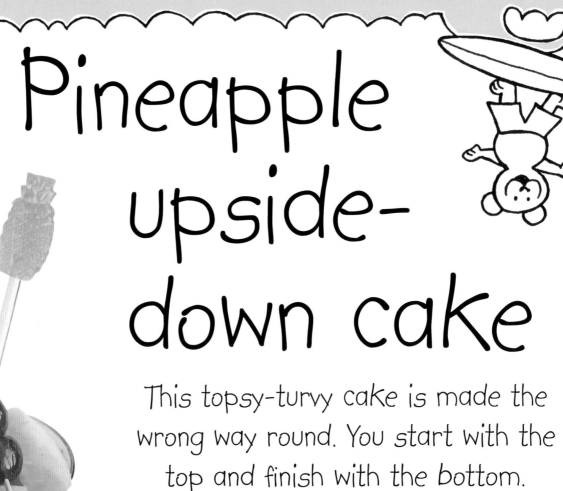

This topsy-turvy cake is made the wrong way round. You start with the top and finish with the bottom.

In an upside-down world would you eat right-side-up cake?

10 minutes to make

25-30 minutes to cook

makes 8 servings

You will need

Basic cake mixture (see p.28)

7 pineapple rings

7 glacé cherries

Equipment

• 20cm (8in) cake tin with loose base • Baking parchment • Large spoon • Serving plate

Making the upside-down cake

This surprising cake makes a yummy dessert or a tropical treat for a party. It's especially delicious with ice cream.

grease the tin

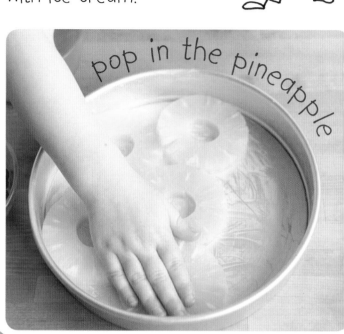

pop in the pineapple

⚠ **1** Heat the oven to 190°C (375°F/Gas 5). Grease the inside of your tin with *butter*, using a piece of baking parchment to spread it.

2 Arrange the pineapple rings on the bottom of the greased tin. If they don't fit without overlapping, you could try trimming them a bit.

Turning the cake upside down

turn the cake over

⚠ **1** When cooked, ask an adult to take the cake out of the oven and let it cool slightly. Then cover it with a plate that's larger than the tin.

⚠ **2** Ask an adult wearing oven gloves to slide one hand under the cake and put another hand on top and then turn the cake in one quick movement.

cover the fruit

3 Put cherries into the centres of the pineapple rings. Make sure their bottoms point down – that's what you'll see when you flip the cake.

4 Carefully spread the cake mixture over the fruit and smooth it out with a large spoon. Bake the cake for 25–30 minutes until golden on top.

ta-da!

3 Carefully remove the outer ring of the cake tin. It may help to jiggle the ring slightly to loosen it before lifting.

4 Lift off the base for the big reveal. Ta-da! You can eat the cake warm or wait for it to cool before cutting it up and serving it.

Cakes

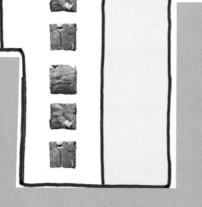

A tower of brownies

Chewy on the outside and gooey on the inside, these brownie blocks are just about perfect.

You will need

250g (9oz) butter, cut into cubes

275g (10oz) dark chocolate (70% cocoa)

275g (10oz) caster sugar

3 large eggs

1 tsp vanilla extract

225g (8oz) plain white flour

75g (2½oz) white chocolate chunks

Equipment

- Saucepan • Wooden spoon
- Large mixing bowl
- Electric mixer or hand whisk
- 23cm (9in) square cake tin
- Baking parchment
- Cooling rack

20 minutes to make

20–25 minutes to cook

makes 36 squares

Making brownies

You'll have lots of fun stirring up this gooey, glossy brownie mixture. Keep a close eye on your brownies as they cook – they should be slightly fudgey in the middle.

I like extra chocolate chunks in my brownies.

melt chocolate

1 Heat the oven to 180°C (350°F/Gas 4). Melt the butter and chocolate over low heat, stirring occasionally. Allow to cool slightly.

2 Using an electric or hand whisk, cream together the sugar, eggs, and vanilla extract until the mixture is fluffy and lighter in colour.

pour in chocolate

3 Pour the chocolate and butter into the egg and sugar mixture bit by bit. Whisk everything together with the electric mixer or hand whisk.

4 Add in a little flour and stir it into the mixture with a wooden spoon. Keep adding and stirring until all the flour is mixed in

sprinkle in the white chocolate chunks

Stir-in substitutes

If you don't like white chocolate, you could try adding in milk chocolate chips, nuts, or raisins.

5 Pour in the white chocolate chunks and fold them into the mixture until they are evenly spread throughout.

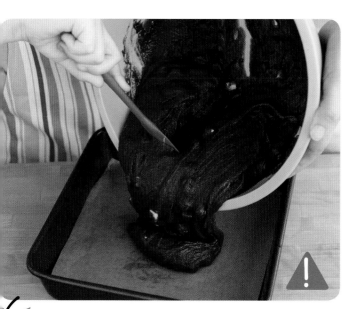

6 Spread the mixture into a lined tin. Bake in the middle of the oven for 20–25 minutes, until the brownies are just set and a bit gooey in the middle.

7 Leave the brownies to cool for 10 minutes in the tin. Then turn out onto a cooling rack. When cool, remove the parchment and cut into squares.

find out more

Why does dough rise?

Water and flour make a stretchy dough to trap the gas bubbles that yeast produces. This makes the dough rise.

Why do we need to Knead?

To make the dough elastic. When it's really stretchy, it can hold the gas bubbles that the yeast makes. As more and more bubbles are made, the dough will start to rise.

1 Push down on the dough with the heel of your hand.

2 Pull the dough, then fold in half.

3 Turn the dough and knead again.

On the rise

Letting the dough rise is called **proving**. This is usually done in a warm place. It lets the yeast get to work before the dough is baked.

What is yeast?

It's a live fungus! Dried yeast is inactive until warm water is added, then it begins to feed on sugars in the bread flour. It releases bubbles as part of the feeding process, causing the dough to rise.

at the start of proving

Push

Push the dough away from you to stretch it.

Pull

Pull it towards you to stretch it before turning.

Catch as many bubbles as you can in your dough.

after 1/2 an hour

The dough continues to trap bubbles, and has risen high up in the bowl.

after an hour

big bubbles

tiny bubbles

pumpkin seeds

poppy seeds

sesame seeds

sunflower seeds

Tear and share bread

The best thing since sliced bread, this homemade loaf is made for sharing. Bring it out to oohs and aahs from friends.

You will need

450g (16oz) strong white bread flour

7g (¼oz) fast-acting (instant) dried yeast

1 tsp salt

1 tsp sugar

250–275ml (8½–9 fl oz) tepid water

milk for brushing

Equipment

• Large mixing bowl • Large spoon
• Tea towel • 23cm (9in) baking tin
• Pastry brush • Wire cooling rack

20 minutes to make (plus 90 minutes rising)

30 minutes to cook

makes 7 large rolls

Making basic bread dough

Making your own bread is easier than you might think. You can use this recipe to make wholemeal bread, too – just replace the white flour with strong wholemeal flour.

pour

1 In a large mixing bowl, combine the flour, salt, sugar, and fast-acting (instant) yeast. Make a well in the centre and pour in the water.

combine

2 Use a spoon and, once the dough becomes too sticky, damp hands to combine all the ingredients together into a ball.

knead

3 Sprinkle some flour on the work surface. Turn out the dough and knead it for 10 minutes, pushing it, stretching it, and folding it until smooth.

cover

4 Put the dough back in the bowl. Cover the bowl with a damp tea towel and leave it in a warm place for an hour or until the dough has doubled in size.

5 Once it has risen "knock back" the dough by punching it lightly in the middle. Then knead it lightly on a floured surface. It's now ready to use.

Making tear and share bread

Smooth moves
Make rolls that are smooth and plump by tucking the sides under, stretching out the top as you do.

shape into rolls

sprinkle
sprinkle
sprinkle

1 Pre-heat the oven to 220°C (425°F/Gas 7). Divide the dough into seven equal-sized pieces, or as many as will fit in your tin. Then shape each piece into a round roll.

brush

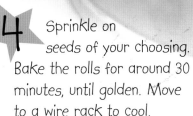

2 Grease the tin with butter and place the rolls snugly inside. Cover the tin with a damp tea towel and leave it to rise for a further 30 minutes.

3 Brush the tops of the rolls with milk using a pastry brush.

4 Sprinkle on seeds of your choosing. Bake the rolls for around 30 minutes, until golden. Move to a wire rack to cool.

 Bread

You will need

Basic bread dough
(see p.50)

Pasta sauce or
tomato purée

Green pepper

Olives

Mushrooms

Sweetcorn

Pepperoni

Basil

Onions

Mozzarella
cheese

Equipment

- Rolling pin • Tablespoon
- Chopping board
- Knife • 2 baking sheets

pizza people

15 minutes to make

10–15 minutes to cook

makes 4 pizzas

and pizza pets

woof, woof!

Making pizza people and pets

Making pizza faces is easy and so much fun. What will yours look like?
It could be a happy person, a silly person – even someone you know.

roll the dough

spread the sauce

1 Pre-heat the oven to 220°C (425°F/Gas 7). Split the dough into four balls. On a floured surface, roll each ball into a round pizza base.

2 Move the bases onto baking sheets. Spread one large tablespoon of sauce on each base. You can use ready-made sauce or tomato purée.

Pizza inspiration

mushroom ears and olive eyes

Woof, woof!

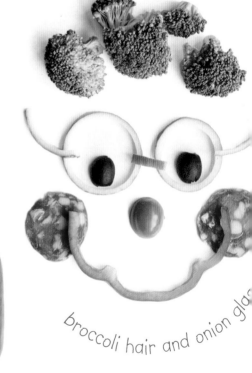
broccoli hair and onion glas

sprinkle cheese

!

make a face

3 Sprinkle grated mozzarella all over the sauce-covered bases. Do the same on the other three pizzas.

4 Make a face on your pizza with your chosen toppings. Bake for 10-15 minutes, until the dough is crisp and the toppings are cooked.

Add salad hair after your pizza is cooked.

Squeak, squeak!

baby corn nose and bacon eyebrows

Making faces

You can use lots of different ingredients to make a pizza face – look on this page for ideas.

Breadsticks

You can also use the bread dough to make crunchy, cheesy breadsticks.

These breadsticks make a great party or picnic food. You can also make plain ones – they're perfect for dipping.

You will need

Basic bread dough (see p.50)

150g (5½oz) grated cheddar cheese

15 minutes to make

10–12 minutes to cook

makes 36 breadsticks

Equipment

- Rolling pin
- Pizza cutter or knife
- Baking tray

⚠ roll out the dough

⚠ cut the dough

1 Heat the oven to 220°C (425°F/Gas 7). Turn out the bread dough onto a floured surface and roll it into a long rectangle.

2 Using a pizza cutter or a knife and starting at the short edge, cut the dough into strips that are roughly 1cm (³/₄in) wide.

roll the strips

sprinkle ⚠

3 Roll each strip under your hands so that it's round all over and transfer to a baking sheet.

4 Sprinkle with cheese and bake for 10-12 minutes. Allow to cool before eating.

Bouncy bread

Jump right in and make this springy Italian-style bread with basil and tomatoes. It's tasty with soups and salads.

You will need

Basic bread dough (see p.50)

A handful of basil leaves

10 cherry tomatoes

50ml (2 fl oz) olive oil

Equipment

- Rolling pin
- Baking tray
- Chopping board
- Knife

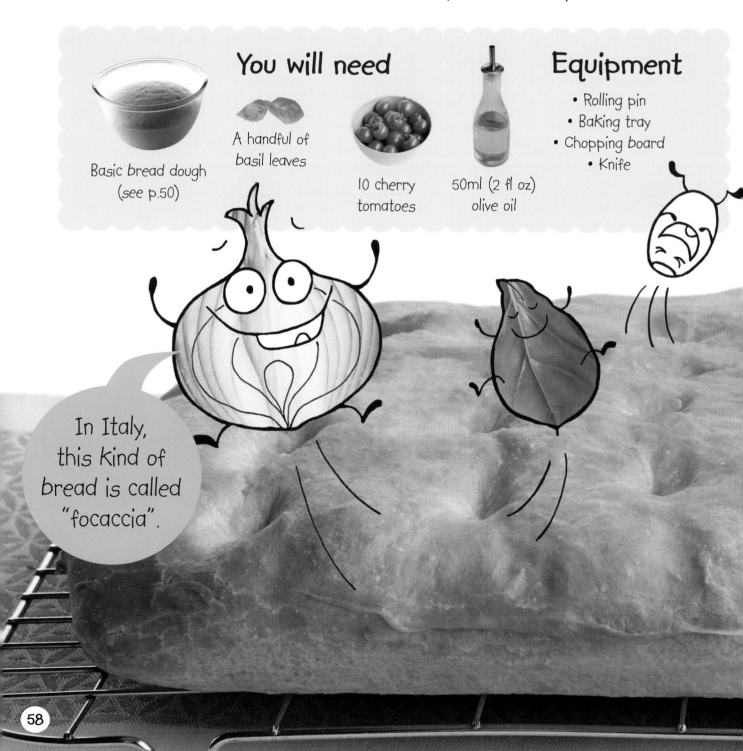

In Italy, this kind of bread is called "focaccia".

I'm going for the high dive.

Olive oil

Topped or not?

This bouncy bread is yummy plain, but you can add all kinds of toppings – tomatoes, olives, onion, even potatoes – for an even tastier treat. Turn the page for tasty topping ideas.

30 minutes to make (plus 30 minutes rising)

25 minutes to cook

makes 9 portions

Making bouncy bread

You can recognize this bread by its dimples. You make them with your finger.
They help the bread rise evenly and provide a place for the olive oil to collect.

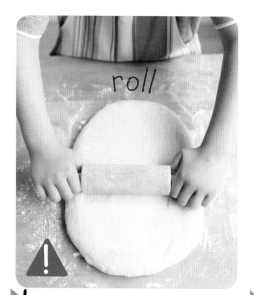

roll

stretch

poke

1 Heat the oven to 220°C (425°F/ Gas 7). Roll the dough into a rectangle to fit your baking tray.

2 Lift the dough onto an oiled baking tray, stretching to fit. Cover it with a towel and leave it to rise for 30 minutes.

3 Next, poke some holes into the dough with your finger. You could also use the handle of a wooden spoon.

Topping ideas

Tomato and basil

Potato and rosemary

decorate

drizzle

4 Now add your toppings. Cut the tomatoes in half and press them into the dough. Press in *basil* leaves between the tomatoes.

5 Drizzle the bread with olive oil, sprinkle on some salt and bake it in the oven for about 25 minutes until the surface is golden brown.

Black olives

Red onion

Top this!
It's easy to make all these different kinds of bread. Just pop on the raw toppings in step 4. They will cook as the bread bakes.

pastry cutters

What makes pastry crumbly?

The best pastry is light, crumbly, and melts in your mouth. To make it, you'll need flour, butter, and a little know-how.

Rubbing in Start by rubbing the butter into the flour. This coats the flour in fat and stops the dough from becoming stretchy.

Resting Handling pastry too much can make it hard. This is why the dough needs a rest after you've made it.

Chef's tip
"Keep yourself and your pastry cool" is the advice given to pastry chefs. This is because heat from your hands can melt the butter in pastry, making it soggy. Keep your pastry cool by chilling it in the fridge and by working quickly so it doesn't have time to warm up.

keeping cool

flour shaker

All floured up
Even chilled pastry can stick to the table. Make rolling easier by dusting flour on your hands, the rolling pin, and your work surface. Pastry that doesn't stick is also quicker to work with.

rolling pin

cooked pastry is crumbly

Rolling out Avoid overworking your pastry by rolling it out quickly and confidently.

Queen of

The queen of tarts she made jam tarts, all on a summer's day...

jam tarts

Make jam tarts fit for a king
or queen using this simple recipe
made up of only four ingredients.

You will need

225g (8oz) plain flour   100g (3½oz) butter   3tbsp water   strawberry jam

Equipment

• Large mixing bowl • Tablespoon
• Clingfilm • Rolling pin • Round pastry
cutter • Bun tin • Small cookie cutters
• Wire cooling rack

30 minutes to make (plus 30 minutes chilling)   15 minutes to cook   makes 24 tarts

Making basic pastry

Making pastry is easier than you might think, but there are a few rules to follow to make sure it turns out as planned. Don't overwork your pastry and remember to give it a rest in the fridge.

rubbing in

pouring

1 Put the butter and flour into a bowl. Use your fingers to rub them together until the mixture looks like breadcrumbs.

2 Add three tablespoons of water to the mixture a little at a time. You can measure it all into a measuring cup first if you like.

wrap and chill

3 Bring the mixture together into a ball using your hands, but be careful not to overwork it. The sides of the bowl should now be clean.

4 Wrap your pastry in clingfilm and chill it in the fridge for half an hour or until firm.

Making jam tarts

rolling

cutting

1 Preheat the oven to 200°C (400°F/Gas 6). Roll out the pastry to 4mm (⅛in) thick.

2 Cut circles with a pastry cutter. Save the scraps to cut shapes for the top.

3 Press the pastry circles into the bun tin. The edges should stick out a bit.

filling

4 Spoon jam into the pastry cases until they are half full. Use small cookie cutters to cut out shapes for the tops from the pastry scraps.

5 Place the pastry shapes on top of the jam. Bake in the oven for about 15 minutes, then transfer to a wire rack to cool.

35 minutes to make

15–20 minutes to cook

makes 12 tarts

Veggie wheels

These savoury tarts are perfect for eating on the go.
Take them on a picnic or pop them in a lunch box.

You will need

Basic pastry
(see p.66)

125g (4¹/₂oz)
sweetcorn

125g (4¹/₂oz)
red pepper, diced

125g (4¹/₂oz)
broccoli

30g (1oz)
grated cheese

2 eggs

100ml (3¹/₂ fl oz)
cream

100ml (3¹/₂ fl oz)
milk

Equipment

- Rolling pin • Pastry cutter
- 6cm (2¹/₂in) round tart tins
- Chopping board • Knife
- Measuring jug
- Fork • Baking tray

Making veggie wheels

Once you know how to make pastry, you'll make these wheels in no time at all. You can eat them warm out of the oven, but they are also tasty cold.

rolling out

1 Preheat the oven to 200°C (400°F/Gas 6). Roll out the pastry to 4mm (⅛in).

2 Cut circles from the pastry with the pastry cutter. You could also use a cup.

3 Lay each pastry circle over a tin. Press it into place so that it fits the tin.

filling

4 Use your hands or a knife to separate the broccoli "trees" from the stem. This makes them easier to fit into the veggie wheels.

5 Fill the pastry cases three-quarters full with sweetcorn, peppers, and broccoli. Move the tins to a baking tray.

beating

6 Beat the eggs together with the milk and cream until evenly mixed.

Ham and cheese wheels

Make these tarts in the same way as the veggie wheels. Just add some chopped cooked ham in Step 5.

pouring

7 Pour the mixture into the cases and sprinkle cheese on top. Bake for 15–20 minutes until the filling sets and allow to cool before serving.

Pastry

Fruit boats

Treats ahoy! Serve these amazing fruit-filled boats as a delicious dessert or teatime treat.

Fruit flotilla

We have used boat-shaped tart tins to make these boats, but you could use round ones, too.

Equipment

• Rolling pin • Boat-shaped tart tins
• Baking parchment • Baking beans or dried beans • Mixing bowl • Wooden spoon • Chopping board • Knife

20 minutes to make

13 minutes to cook

makes 16 tarts

You will need

Basic pastry (*see* p.66)

150g (5½oz) mascarpone cheese

2tbsp icing sugar

½tsp vanilla extract

Blackberries

Peaches

Blueberries

Strawberries

Kiwis

Raspberries

Making fruit boats

These pastry shells are baked without any filling.
This is called "baking blind". We fill them with special baking beans
to help them keep their shape, but you could also use dried beans.

1 Roll out the pastry and cut it into rectangles that are bigger than the tins. Lay a rectangle of pastry over each tin and press it in.

2 Roll a rolling pin across the top of each tin to cut off the edges. Preheat the oven to 200°C (400°F/Gas 6).

3 Cut out a piece of baking parchment to fit each boat. Fill them with beans and bake for 10 minutes. Remove the beans and paper and bake for 3 more minutes.

mixing

4 Allow the pastry shells to cool before popping them out of their cases with the help of a knife. In a bowl, mix the cheese, sugar, and vanilla together until smooth.

cutting

5 Wash the berries and fruit that you're using. Cut the bigger fruit into shapes that will fit your pastry boats. Make sure you cut a few tall shapes to use as sails.

Watch out – here come pie-rates!

6 Fill the cooled pastry shells with the cheese mixture and position the fruit on top. Treats ahoy!

Chicken turnovers

These chicken and potato turnovers contain a mini-meal in a pastry parcel. They are perfect for buffets and picnics.

You will need

Basic pastry
(see p.66)

50g (2oz) potato

50g (2oz)
sweet potato

115g (4oz) cooked
chicken (1 breast)

40g (1½oz)
cream cheese

2 spring onions, chopped
1 tbsp chopped parsley

1 egg,
beaten

Equipment

• Chopping board • Knife • Mixing bowl • Wooden spoon • Rolling pin • 11cm (4½in) pastry cutter • Fork • Pastry brush • Baking tray • Wire cooling rack

Pasties

You can also make bigger turnovers, called pasties, perfect for lunch on the go. Use a small plate to cut out bigger pastry circles and prepare as directed.

20 minutes to make

25-30 minutes to cook

makes 6-8 turnovers

Cheep, cheep!

Making chicken turnovers

These parcels are made with cooked chicken but raw vegetables.
In the oven, the vegetables cook in the cream cheese sauce. Yum!

1 Preheat the oven to 200°C (400°F/Gas 6). Chop the potato, sweet potato, and chicken into 1cm (½in) cubes.

2 Mix together the cream cheese, spring onion, and parsley. Add the other ingredients to the bowl.

stir

3 Stir all the ingredients together, making sure that everything is evenly coated in the cream cheese mixture.

cut out

4 Roll out the pastry. Cut out circles using a round pastry cutter.

spoon filling

5 Put a large spoonful of filling into the middle of each pastry circle.

brush

6 Use a pastry brush to brush egg along one half of each pastry circle.

fold
press
stick

Crimping
To close your pastry parcels tightly, squeeze the dough together with your fingers all along the edge.

7 Fold over the pastry circles. Use your fingers to crimp the edges. Pierce the tops a few times with a fork.

8 Move the turnovers to a baking tray and brush them with egg. Bake them in the oven for 25–30 minutes, then cool on a rack.

Each parcel contains a tasty meal.

Index

Now it's time to clean and do the washing up.

Acknowledgements

With thanks to: Wendy Horobin and Anne Hildyard for additional editing and James Mitchem for proofreading.

With special thanks to the models: Abi Arnold, Emily Fox, Olive Hole, Cassius Moore Cockrell, Eleanor Moore-Smith, Kaylan Patel, Edward Phillips, Dylan Tannazi, Isabella Thompson